"Dedicated to the Bomber Command"

About the author

Gwyn Elwyn Evans was born on Good Friday, April 2nd 1920.
In 1939 he became a Radio Officer in the Merchant Navy, Cardiff
before joining the Royal Airforce in Bomber Command.
Of the nine men who went to serve in Bomber Command
during World War II, he was the only one to return to Blaengarw.

He currently lives with his partner of 37 years, Joan.
He has two sons, Robert and Tony.

1. World At War

BOMBS GONE

Bombs Gone!
Turn back on course and fly away,
And live to fly another day.
The bombs are gone, and Johnny's gone.
A ball of orange flame--- it fell,
And Johnny --- well, he's gone to hell.

THE BOMBERS MOON

There are squadrons that are flying
When the autumn winds are sighing
And the bomber's moon is riding in the sky

Can't you hear their engines roaring
As together they are soaring
In the same old way they did in times gone by?

Can't you feel your soul returning
To the nights when youth was burning
And that same old moon invited you to fly?

Now that roar is fast receding
Can't you feel your heart a' bleeding
For those half forgotten friends who will not die?

Can't you hear your friends explaining
As the moon is gently waning
That you cannot join those squadrons up on high?

Though they'll always be a' flying
When the autumn winds are sighing
You will never join those squadrons passing by.

BOMBER COMMAND

In skies above an alien land
They gave their lives------
By the thousand
Tens of thousands;
Fifty six thousand;
My comrades-------
The flower of Britain's youth.
When I am gone
Let it be said of me
"He flew with this illustrious band
-------------Bomber command."

BOMBER PILOT

Each night you tamed the kingdom of the dark,
And took your place among the twinkling stars.
You knew friendship of the lonely cloud,
Until the moon, resentful of your power,
Betrayed you to a silent, unseen foe.
Now---in the velvet night you still remain,
But only as a shadow of your former self
A shadow --- silhouetted on a cloud

THE PRISONER OF WAR'S – FAREWELL TO NICOTINE

You served me well my faithful friend.
Auf wiedersehn, this is the end.
Fate has decreed that we must part.
Ah nicotine! You break my heart.

I smoked you medium, strong and mild,
Players, Capstan, Woodbine Wild.
Abdullah's, Junaks, Caporals
Were all the very best of pals.

But time it is we said goodbye,
Geneva well at last is dry,
So with my last and only fag
I'll take my longest, sweetest drag.

My fingers burn, the end is near.
I've had my time at last I fear,
And now the end I've thrown away
Until we meet another day.

"VERGISSMEINNICHT."

"Vergissmeinnicht," she said
---forget me not.
As if I could
When shy the flower blooms
I still recall
Her last goodbye.
"Vergissmeinnicht", she cried,
As Auschwitz bound
The transport rolled
Fast stealing her away.
"Liebchen. Liebchen.
Vergissmeinnicht"---
While blue the flower blows
I never will.
As if I could
---as if I ever would.

"STICK IT THE WELCH"

"Stick it the Welch"
The cry rang out
As round about they fell
---At Chemin De Dames,
Near Chivy on the Aisne.
"Stick it the Welch,"
And this they did,
Before the sweeping fire
Of hidden guns---
Singing a song of hate
And swift oblivion``` `.
To silence the song,
Haggard led the charge,
To fall, and falling cried
"Stick it the Welch,"
And so they did---
Dai, Ianto, Twm and Will,
And as they bled
The valleys all were weeping
For Fathers and Sons,
Brothers too,
Who would not be returning.

Although the memory might fade,
Proud in Valhalla's scared halls
That poignant cry will linger on
----------"Stick it the Welch"

MAMETZ WOOD 1916

"Largest wood on the Somme," they said
--- had to be taken.
Were you there when we counted the dead
--- the forsaken?
Mown down like corn before the unrelenting blade
--- fathers and sons,
Caught in that stuttering, lethal enfilade
--- of spiteful guns.
Were you there when we buried the dead
--- where they fell?
No time for tears, silently, prayers unsaid
--- no tolling bell.
We gained the prize, but at an awful cost
--- death was the winner,
For at Mametz the flower of Wales was lost
--- saint and sinner,
And there they'll lie throughout eternity
--- where they bled,
Their deeds a half remembered memory
--- the valiant dead.

LAST NIGHT

Last night he turned and looked at me,
And then I knew that he was mad.
I knew though I could hardly see
For tears that blurred, and made me sad.

I knew because his eyes looked out
At weird things they could not see,
And when he spoke, without a doubt
He said the strangest things to me.

We two in this cold prison cell
Had shared each laugh and every tear.
We suffered in a man–made hell
Where happiness was turned to fear.

We knew the wild fantastic flights
Of daylight's hopeful, hopeless schemes,
And in the hollow, haunting nights
Our fevered minds were racked by dreams.

These things we'll never share again,
Because his poor weak mind is free
To roam above the realm of pain
Where my poor mind must ever be.

2. The Ones I Love

TO JOAN

I loved you through the nights and through the days,
A hundred thousand different ways.
I love you still, and through eternity
My love will last for all to see.
A beacon burning, blazing in the night
Illuminating all in sight.
My love will live in every scented flower
And in the fresh'ning April shower.
In every breeze that stirs the autumn leaf
My love will live beyond belief.
Twill lives and laugh in every singing stream
In every thought, in every dream
Can words express the depth of such a love?
---Emblazoned in the stars above?

MY MOTHER (1)

Two shy brown eyes,
A smile that's wise,
A voice so sweet,
Such tiny feet,
--- my mother.

MY SON

That photograph!
My son you know.
Played for the first fifteen,
Scored the winning try against St Paul's,
Before the war.
Those medals on the shelf below--------?
Did I tell you he played for the first fifteen?
Against St. Paul's
I did!
I'm sorry.

MY FATHER

My father was a singing man,
Before the First World War.
He toured the halls of Moss and Stoll;
And many venues more.

Although he never topped the bill,
No matter how he tried,
His voice was honey sweet you know,
His listeners always cried,

He sang Macushla and Because,
The Song of Songs as well,
Vienna City of my Dreams,
And Tosti's last Farewell.

One sad old song my mother loved,
My sister loved it too---
Of the rose that bloomed in Picardy,
In the hush of a silv'ry dew.

When with the 24'th of Foot
In khaki uniform
His singing brought back thoughts of home
Wherever he 'd perform

And in the lean and hungry years
Of poverty and pain
With naught save dignity and pride
He sang his songs again

He left behind a sweeter song
Than those they sing today
And though he's gone it lingers on
It will not fade away

MY LADY

My lady when she's dressed in grey
  Doth seem austere in every way.

My lady when she's dressed in white
  Doth seem the essence of delight.

My lady when she's dressed in green
  Doth seem as stately as a queen.

My lady when she's dressed in wine
  Doth seem to me divine.

My lady stripped of all her clothes
  Doth seem as lovely as a rose.

MY MOTHER (2)

One hundred years and four she lived,
My Mother --- rest her soul.
She had such kind and gentle ways,
A heart of pure gold.

When opportunities for girls
Were few and far between
She plied the craft of tailoress
On Singer's old machine.

She had a fine contralto voice,
So soft and oh so low.
Turned down a chance to tour the States.
Just didn't want to know.

At the Ball, she danced away
The Waltz and the Veleta,
With grace and elegance, and style,
To music then much sweeter.

But in grey, unfriendly days
She kept in the wolf at bay,
By sewing deep into the night
So we could pay our way.

She's with my Father now I know,
Wherever that may be.
Better parents never were,
Their like no more we'll see.

3. Finality Of Life

FINALITY

I thought of you last night.
In the dark before the dawn
I thought of you,
And wanted you
Oh how I wanted you!
In the cool of the night
I wanted your warmth beside me;
Wanted the scent of your hair
Falling across my cheek;
Wanted your gentle touch
And sweet caress.
Oh how I wanted you!
But came the dawn,
And with its light reality,
For you had gone-----------
Forever.

WHEN I AM GONE

When I am dead and gone, remember me---
I lived and laughed and loved and touched the stars;
Knew love's first kiss, and many kisses more;
Knew sorrow, death, and deep and dark despair.

I sought the rainbow's fabled crock of gold,
But I sought in vain, for gold there never was.
Instead the crock was full of discontent
Of words unsaid, and wishes unfulfilled.

On silver wings I soared above the clouds,
And stood alone in awe of time and space.
I questioned all, but answer never found.
God's infinite a mystery remained.

I sailed the seas to strange uncharted isles,
And heard the surf break on their pebbled shores.
I sang the songs of many different lands,
And marvelled at man's weird and wanton ways.

I plumbed the depths, and scaled the topmost peaks
To watch the sun desert the western sky.
I searched for truth, but truth eluded me
Till I found wisdom, love, and freedom unconfined.

I dreamed my dreams, built castles in the air,
And played the fool, and sometimes played the man.
When I am gone will you remember this---?
I lived, and laughed, and loved and touched the stars.

LIFE

When I was one and twenty
I heard an old man say
"Don't waste your time in dreaming,
But live for each today"

Now I am one and eighty,
And life has passed me by,
I rue the day I doubted him
To beg the question why?

Had I but grasped the nettle
To smell the scented flower,
And fill o overflowing
The unrelenting hour!

My days would be contented,
All would be sublime,
I'd cherish every memory
Until the end of time.

Alas my days are full of woe,
Of sorrow and regret;
Loves lost and wishes unfulfilled
---Of things I'd best forget

Don't hesitate to pluck the rose,
To sip the sparkling wine,
For life is meant for living
Not wasting---just like mine.

MORTALITY

Down the road this morning,
I saw his name upon the post.
I did not know that he had gone,
But there it was--- Dan Jones,
Friday next at Coity "Crem"
Two thirty in the afternoon.
I'll be there. I owe him that.
I knew him once see.
He had been a friend---long ago,
Not close, but close enough.
Of late we'd grown apart,
And now he's gone.
On Friday next we'll gather
To bid him fond farewell---
His friends, our number dwindling.
Too soon I'll stand-alone.
Who'll mourn for me?
An icon of the past.
This morning on the funeral post
I saw his name--- and my mortality.

ONLY ME.

When at the closing of day
I fall upon my knees to pray,
I thank the Lord that I am me,
For is who I want to be.
Composed of faith, of hope and love
I fit myself just like a glove.
Someone else would not feel right---
Too big, too small, too slack, too tight.
With me I always feel at ease,
I only have myself to please.
In me you get just what you see,
And me I'd rather be than thee.

LIFE'S CUP

Half empty now the cup that was half full,
And dust the dreams, which held the futures bright.
Long gone the leaves which decked the tree of life,
And sad the thought of winters chilling bright,.

Regrets--- the hope which one uplifted me
To fill the heart with rare and pure delight
Have soured the wine remaining in the cup,
And brought me to a mean and sorry plight.

Could I recall those moments from the past?
When skies were blue, without a cloud in sight:
When days were long and lazy in the sun,
Then cares and troubles would be put to flight.

But wishes are the dreams we dream day by day,
Vain promises which flourish with the light,
To fade before the advent of the dark
When all is silent in the stillness of the night.

Would that the cup once more was brimming o'er
With bubbles sparkling at the rim, I might
Again imbibe the sweet white wine of life
Before I bid you all my last and sad good-night.

THE LIGHT OF MY LIFE

You are the light of my life,
Illuminating the darkest corners of the soul,
Where dwell despair and doubt?
Anxiety and fear.
And when the spirit wavers,
As oft it will,
Your light burns ever brighter,
Driving out the demons of the night.
Yours is the light that never fails.

*Gwyn's Uncle Evan Davy Evans and Aunt Rose
circa 1919/1920*

Daniel Thomas Davies and Maggie Meredith
(Gwyn's Grandparents)

Old Junior School - 1927

4. Fantasy Moments

IN DREAMS

In dreams I walk a golden mile,
Then rest upon a crooked stile
To watch the evening sun go down
Over the hill behind the town.

I dream of tea, and cakes, and ale,
The skylark and the nightingale,
If cricket on the village green,
And all the things I've ever seen.

Awake, I see a host of stars
Twinkling through the prison bars,
And then I realise with pain,
I dreamed my dreams but all in vain

I dream, I wake, I cry and then
I dream and cry and wake again,
For each new day will always be
The same as yesterday for me

MAGIC MOMENTS

If you could call back time
To live one moment from the past,
What would it be ----------?
That first, sweet stolen kiss,
Or what came after,
When you lost your girlish laughter;
Those hushed and tender words
I do --- I do,
As you promised to be true;
Or would it be when first
With the blissful sigh
You heard your newborn baby cry?
With memories such as these,
And more beside,
How possibly can you decide?
Better by far you yet
Can capture
Each magic moment's early rapture.

THE LONELY DRAGONFLY

An iridescent wisp of magic
Flittering o'er the water's edge.
Departing here and darting there,
Seeking out his erstwhile mate.
Seeking, seeking---ever seeking,
Darting hither, darting thither,
Ever seeking---never finding.
Flittering on the breeze
That softly stirs the reeds
Around the water's edge

GIFTS OF THE MAGI

Casper, Melchior, Balthazar,
Kings who've traveled from afar,
Following God's guiding light
Through the darkness of the night.

Coming on that lonely inn
Where an infant free from sin
Cradled on sweet scented hay
In the stable manger lay.

To Mary mild they said behold---
Frankincense divinity,
Myrrh a sign of pain and sorrow,
Portent of a sad tomorrow.

Through the night they vigil keep,
While the child lay fast asleep,
But with the dawning of the day
Silently they steal away.

Across the desert's burning sands
Back to strange enchanted lands,
There to spread the word of love,
The gift bestowed by heaven above.

FIAT LUX.

God said, "Let there be light"
And beauty was born -----------
From the blush of the first red dawn
To the gold of the last sad sunset
Beauty will endure, everywhere.
In the sound of raindrops
Kissing the scented petals
Of Summer's fading roses
Beauty will last. As long as life itself
God's beauty will survive, all around
God creates, man desecrates.
True beauty is lasting, that of man
In transient, passing with the fashion,
Leaving desolation and decay.
Like the cobweb, silver dropt with morning dew,
Real beauty will prevail, until the end of time.
When God said "Let there be light"
There was light, and beauty was born.

NB Fiat Lux - Let there be light.

THE JUDAS KISS

In the garden called Gethsemene,
On the Passover,
By Cedron brook, he was betrayed.
The son of man.
Betrayed with a kiss from Judas,
Flame haired Judas.
For thirty pieces of silver
He was betrayed---
To the priests and Pharisees,
The Son of man,
By Judas, keeper of the purse,
The trusted one.
Filled with remorse, he hanged himself,
Flame haired Judas,
From the tree thereafter called
The Judas tree ---
The Judas kiss and the Judas tree,
Symbols since of treachery.

MY NUT BROWN GYPSY MAID.

Sing heigh for my nut-brown gypsy maid
With sparkling eyes,
Flashing thighs,
Teeth like pearls,
And windswept curls.
Sing ho for my wanton gypsy jade.
Sing heigh, sing ho, as away we go
On the rolling road to nowhere.

Sing heigh for my wayward gypsy maid,
Sara's child,
Growing child,
Crossing palms,
And giving charms.
Sing ho for my feckless gypsy jade.
Sing heigh, sing ho, sing sweet and low,
As we travel the road to nowhere.

Sing heigh for my roving gypsy maid,
Silver spangled,
Ringed and bangled,
Fortune telling,
Trinket selling.
Sing ho for my winsome gypsy jade.
Sing heigh; sing ho, song soft and slow,
As we bid good-bye to nowhere

IN SAECULA SAECULORUM

I stood upon the threshold of the beckoning dawn
To watch the flickering stars forsake the velvet night,
And wondered how and when eternity was born,
And why God used those magic words "Let there be light"

I looked at stars which died a million years before,
Stars numbered as the desert's myriad grains of sand.
Stars strewn throughout forever and forever more,
As if by chance it seemed, but yet so carefully planned.

Then rosy hued Aurora swept the stars away,
And drew a veil of blue across the morning sky,
Above where fly the skylark and the screeching jay,
Beyond the lonely cloud that slowly passes by.

I saw where there was no beginning nor no end;
I saw no day, no night, no Summer, Winter, Spring nor Fall.
A mystery that none can ever comprehend,
Save God alone, the orchestrator of it all.

N.B In Saecula Saeculorum means for ever and ever

UNKNOWN WARRIOR

Known unto God alone,
He who lies here sleeping,
Beneath this simple stone
Amid the poppies weeping,
Felt once the kiss of sun,
Heard the wild wind sighing,
But now the battle won
In foreign field he's lying.
Upon the Judgement day,
When Gabriel's horn is sounding,
God will have his way,
And grant him grace abounding.

5. The Valleys Is Where My Heart Is

LLANGEINOR ARMS

Close to the ancient church of Cein,
An early Celtic saint,
You'll find a small, secluded inn,
Hospitable and quaint.

Standing 'neath the brooding trees
Whispering nearby,
You gaze upon a scene below
Most pleasing to the eye.

Where once Black Evans mill wheel turned
In Ogwr's singing stream,
There's nothing but a memory;
Nothing but a dream.

And yet the name still lingers on---
Melyn Ifan Ddu
Blackmill as we all know it now,
As such 'twill ever be

Behind the inn, the churchyard slopes,
It's gravestones cold and grey,
Some so old their epitaphs
With time are worn away.

I wonder if the monks of old
Who farmed the Abbot's land?
Spectral chant within the church
The church de Londres planned

The only ghost within the inn,
The spirit of good will---
Cool on sultry summer days,
Warm whene'er it's chill.

Summer, Winter, Autumn, Spring,
Whenever at the Arms,
A willing victim you will be,
Seduced by all its charm.

BUT WILL THE DEBT BE PAID?

Where swoops the buzzard on the hill
The pit wheels turned of yore.
Where swim the shy and speckled trout
The stream ran black before.

Yet now that grey has turned to green,
And coal no longer reigns,
A shadow of the past comes back
To haunt us once again.

The cough, the spit, the sudden gasp,
And rasping fight for breath
Of those who spent there lives below
--- the slow, the painful death.

As times goes by and men pass on
The ghost will then be laid,
The cursed dust will kill no more
But will the debt be paid?

PRYSOR PUGH.

The Reverend Pugh is all a'fluster,
Rant and rave and cant and bluster.
Even when he kneels to pray
His voice is like an ass's bray.
His sigh is as the worth wind blowing;
His whisper like a cockerel crowing,
And when in spate, apart from boring,
He sounds just like a lion roaring.
As a road without a bend
His sermons never seem to end.
His bombast makes the senses numb,
I wish the Lord would strike him dumb.

YOU WON'T FORGET THE VALLEY

You may talk about the wonders of a score of foreign lands:
The Parthenon in Athens, and Rio's golden sands;
The pyramids of Gizeh, with the Sphinx not far away;
The Taj Mahal by moonlight, and the gems of old Cathay.

You may shout about the glory of the Road to Mandalay;
Of the evenings spent in drunken bliss in the brothels of Marseilles.
You may rant about the marvels of the seven hills of Rome,
But you won't forget the valley; you won't forget your home.

You may boast about the things you've done in countries far away;
Of the beauty of the girls you've kissed in 'Frisco and Bombay.
There was Tiger Lil in Cairo, Margarita in Brazil,
Natasha in old Moscow, and Maria in Seville.

Perhaps you've danced the hula with Marama of the Isles
Or the Rumba with Lolita, half-caste girl of many wiles.
You may have danced the Csardas in stately Budapest,
And listened to the gypsy bands that play in Bucharest.

You may have seen the Hareems of the sheiks of Isfahan,
Or taken tea with geisha girls in fairy-land Japan
Perhaps you've known the houris who haunt the Shalimar,
And talked with native slave girls in the land of Zanzibar.

You may know leggy Broadway girls, who wear revealing scanties,
And dusky Harlem beauty queens who e'en forget their panties,
And then again, you may have known the gay Parisian ladies
Whose pasts so dark would even bar their entry into Hades.

Of all the lovely glamour girls you've known from east to west,
You yet must know that valley girls are still the very best
You'll not forget those girls at home will kiss and never tell.
You'll not forget those girls at home are beautiful as well.

You wont forget the purple splash of heather on the hill,
The magic of the morning mist, the music of the rill.
You wont forget the hiraeth of the golden song of Wales,
Or the welcome that awaits you in the mountains and the vales

SPRING

When Spring comes dancing down the lane
To cast off Winter's counterpane,
His singing stirs the sleeping Earth,
And fills the land with wakening mirth.

Where'er his twinkling feet do stray
The newborn violets will play,
And children when they hear his song
Will shout and dance the whole day long.

He'll bring the birds back to the trees,
And put the perfume in the breeze.
And then to keep alive the flowers
He'll bring the fresh'ning April showers.

He'll drive away the cloudy skies,
And put the laughter in your eyes,
Then when his merry rout in through,
He'll bring the Summer unto you.

ANGHARAD RHYS

Before she crept into his life
To be his awful wedded wife,
Angharad Rhys, the sexton's bride,
Had cast her net both far and wide,
To play the field and sip honey
Until she settled for his money.
How wrong she was, for he's flat broke.
Of course she doesn't see the joke,
But as was said in days of old---
All that glitters is not gold.

BRONWEN

Ah Bronwen!
You were lovely then,
With the cool sweet wind
Rippling the tendrils
Of your sun-gold hair;
With the music of the waters
Trickling when you spoke;
With the flush of tears
Brimming the violets of your eyes.
You were lovely
--- and I loved you then.

THE ICE CREAM MAKERS.

From Bardi they came,
In sunny Italy-------
The ice cream makers:
Bracchi, Moruzzi,
Strinatti and the rest,
Seeking an El Dorado
In the valley towns of Wales.
In the warmth of their cafes
We plotted, planned, and schemed,
And dreamed.
They are with us yet ---
Sidoli, Fulgoni,
Rabaiotti and the others
--- the ice cream makers
From Bardi,
In sunny Italy.

TWO LOVES HAVE I

On pale and slender limbs the bluebells dance
To April's sprightly song.
Planted long since by one I loved so well,
Who loved me in return
Her life too short---she left me on my own
To weep my silent tears,
Until by chance a new love came my way,
A tender love and true.
But still---when the bluebells dance to April's song,
My old love's dancing too.

THE WIND

The western wind is full of flowers,
Laughing girls and golden hours.

The southern wind is like the wine
Made from the lush Italian vine.

The eastern wind though winters past
Is still a cold and icy blast

The northern wind is full of woe,
Because it brings the chill snow.

And yet the wind can play the fool,
To blow without reason, rhyme or rule.

GIVE ME ALL THESE

Give me a roof above my head.
Give me a wife to share my bed.
Give me a garden filled with flowers.
Give me the fresh'ning April showers.
Give me a golden sun at noon.
Give me by night the silver moon.
Give me the love song of a bird.
Give me a kind and gentle word.
Give me all these, and I shall be
The richest man in God's country.

6. A Sense of Christmas

THE FIRST NOWELL

*Sing soft for Jesus now is sleeping
While the angels watch are keeping.
At the inn the wine is flowing
Round about cool winds are blowing
As the dawn above is breaking,
Mary mild her rest is taking.
Three wise men their prayers are saying,
In the stall an ass is braying
With the shepherds homage paying,
From the fold the sheep are straying.
Following the noise they're making,
The holy babe will soon be waking
To the sound of cattle lowing,
And the early cooks a crowing
As the stable wakes from sleeping
Angels still their watch are keeping.
Thus it was that Christmas morn
When the King of Kings was born.*

CHRISTMAS WISHES

Christmas bells and Christmas candles,
Red the berry on the tree,
Yule log burning, thoughts returning,
Of the friends no more we'll see.

Christmas cheer and Christmas greetings,
Kisses 'neath the mistletoe.
Memories of an infant cradled
In a manger long ago

Christmas joys and Christmas sorrows,
Voices on the mid-night clear,
Singing songs of expectation
For a future without fear.

Christmas hopes and Christmas wishes,
Dreams of home from far away,
Childhood prayers all but forgotten
For a bright new Christmas Day.

CHRISTMAS VERSE FOR S-----.

On this one day of all the year
I wish you luck, good health, and cheer.
I wish your life will ever be
A page of gold for all to see.
I wish that you'll be kind and true,
That god will always comfort you.
I wish that when you are a man
You'll always do the best you can,
And listen lad, another thing---
I wish I was a rich old king,
For then I'd buy you all the toys
That brings such fun to girls and boys.
Alas! a king I'll never be,
And so the toys you'll never see.
Instead I send you all my love,
And every wish that's penned above.